A Note from
Mary Pope Osborne About the

MAGIC TREE HOUSE®

FACT TRACKERS

When I write Magic Tree House® adventures, I love including facts about the times and places Jack and Annie visit. But when readers finish these adventures, I want them to learn even more. So that's why my husband, Will, and my sister, Natalie Pope Boyce, and I write a series of nonfiction books that are companions to the fiction titles in the Magic Tree House® series. We call these books Fact Trackers because we love to track the facts! Whether we're researching dinosaurs, pyramids, Pilgrims, sea monsters, or cobras, we're always amazed at how wondrous and surprising the real world is. We want you to experience the same wonder we do—so get out your pencils and notebooks and hit the trail with us. You can be a Magic Tree House® Fact Tracker, too!

Mary Pope Osborne

Here's what kids, parents, and teachers have to say about the Magic Tree House® Fact Trackers:

"They are so good. I can't wait for the next one. All I can say for now is prepare to be amazed!" —Alexander N.

"I have read every Magic Tree House book there is. The [Fact Trackers] are a thrilling way to get more information about the special events in the story." —John R.

"These are fascinating nonfiction books that enhance the magical time-traveling adventures of Jack and Annie. I love these books, especially *American Revolution*. I was learning so much, and I didn't even know it!" —Tori Beth S.

"[They] are an excellent 'behind-the-scenes' look at what the [Magic Tree House fiction] has started in your imagination! You can't buy one without the other; they are such a complement to one another." —Erika N., mom

"Magic Tree House [Fact Trackers] took my children on a journey from Frog Creek, Pennsylvania, to so many significant historical events! The detailed manuals are a remarkable addition to the classic fiction Magic Tree House books we adore!" —Jenny S., mom

"[They] are very useful tools in my classroom, as they allow for students to be part of the planning process. Together, we find facts in the [Fact Trackers] to extend the learning introduced in the fictional companions. Researching and planning classroom activities, such as our class Olympics based on facts found in *Ancient Greece and the Olympics*, help create a genuine love for learning!" —Paula H., teacher

Magic Tree House®
Fact Tracker
VIKINGS

A nonfiction companion to
Magic Tree House® #15:
Viking Ships at Sunrise

by Mary Pope Osborne
and Natalie Pope Boyce

illustrated by Carlo Molinari

A STEPPING STONE BOOK™
Random House 🏠 New York

The Magic Tree House Fact Tracker series was formerly known as the Magic
Tree House Research Guide series.

Visit us on the Web!
SteppingStonesBooks.com
MagicTreeHouse.com

Educators and librarians, for a variety of teaching tools, visit us at
RHTeachersLibrarians.com

Library of Congress Cataloging-in-Publication Data
Osborne, Mary Pope.
Vikings / by Mary Pope Osborne and Natalie Pope Boyce ; illustrated by Carlo
Molinari.
p. cm.—(Magic tree house fact tracker)
"A nonfiction companion to Magic Tree House #15: Viking Ships at Sunrise."
"A Stepping Stone book."
Audience: K to grade 3.
ISBN 978-0-385-38638-8 (trade) —ISBN 978-0-385-38639-5 (lib. bdg.) —
ISBN 978-0-385-38640-1 (ebook)
1. Vikings—Juvenile literature. I. Boyce, Natalie Pope. II. Molinari, Carlo,
illustrator. III. Osborne, Mary Pope. Viking Ships at Sunrise. IV. Title.
DL66.O83 2015 948'.022—dc23 2015008568

Printed in the United States of America
10 9 8 7 6 5 4 3 2 1

This book has been officially leveled by using the F&P Text Level Gradient™
Leveling System.

For Robert Sorenson, our favorite Viking

Historical Consultants:

JONAS WELLENDORF, Assistant Professor of Old Norse,
and ROSIE TAYLOR, graduate student, Department of Scandinavian Studies,
University of California, Berkeley

Education Consultant:

HEIDI JOHNSON, language acquisition and science education specialist,
Bisbee, Arizona
Special thanks to the great team at Random House: Mallory Loehr,
Paula Sadler, Jenna Lettice, Heather Palisi, Carlo Molinari for his wonderful
art, and as always to our superb editor, Diane Landolf

VIKINGS

Contents

Dear Readers,

In <u>Viking Ships at Sunrise,</u> we went to a monastery in the Middle Ages. Viking raiders often attacked monasteries and stole their treasures. After we got home, we wanted to know who the Vikings were and why they attacked so many places.

We started reading books from the library. What we found out about these fierce and brave people amazed us. The Vikings lived in what is now Norway, Sweden, and Denmark, but they sailed long distances across the sea. They were some of the greatest sailors the world has ever seen. In fact, they sailed to North America long before Columbus ever did!

We also checked out a few websites and learned about how Vikings lived. We found pictures of weapons, houses, ships, and graves that gave us clues. We found out what they wore and what foods they ate. We even read stories about their gods and goddesses. There was so much to learn!

So put notebooks and pencils in your backpacks and let's sail off to the land of the Vikings!

Jack
Annie

1

Vikings

The Vikings are coming! The Vikings are coming!

A thousand years ago, these were the scariest words people could possibly hear. Everyone living along the coasts of England and France ran like crazy when Viking warships sailed into view.

They had reason to be afraid. When the Vikings attacked, they burned down buildings, killed people, took captives, and stole treasures.

These warriors came from different tribes in what are now Norway, Sweden, and Denmark. Powerful kings and chieftains ruled the tribes. They often fought with one another. But in the ninth century, the Vikings began looking for riches far from home.

The Vikings' Homeland

Norway, Sweden, and Denmark are in northern Europe. These countries are in a region called Scandinavia. The coast of Scandinavia is on the cold Baltic and North Seas.

The area has large forests and rugged mountains. There are also lakes, rivers, and flat plains. Because most Vikings lived near water, they were great sailors and boatbuilders.

Scandinavia has many beautiful fjords (fee-ORDZ) along the coast where the ocean runs in between high cliffs.

Winters in much of Scandinavia are long and cold. Since the soil tends to be rocky, farming is hard. During the time of the Vikings, there were too many people in Scandinavia and not enough ways to make a living.

The Lindisfarne Raid

In AD 793, Christian monks were living in a monastery on an island off the coast of England. The island was called Lindisfarne (LIN-dis-farn). For over a hundred years, the monks had spent their time reading the Bible and praying there. People thought of Lindisfarne as a *sacred* place.

Sacred means holy or religious.

The monastery had a lot of treasures. Gold and silver crosses, cups, plates, and candlesticks glittered on the altars. There were also beautiful Bibles decorated with precious stones.

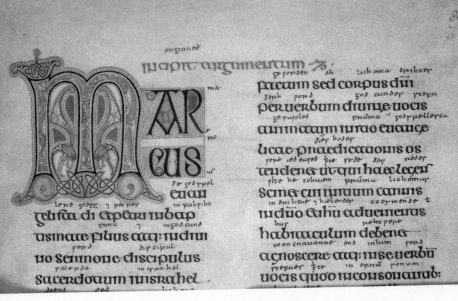

Around AD 700, the monks made a beautiful copy of four books of the Bible called the Lindisfarne Gospels.

On June 8, AD 793, several Viking warships appeared in the waters off Lindisfarne. Men jumped from them and raced up to the monastery. As they ran, they yelled and waved battle-axes over their heads.

There were probably three ships and about 120 men.

17

The monks fled for their lives. The raiders killed many without mercy and captured others to sell as slaves.

Then they smashed down doors and grabbed every precious object they could find. When the Vikings left, the monastery was in ruins and its treasures were gone.

Age of the Vikings

The Lindisfarne raid began a time called the Age of the Vikings. It lasted for almost three hundred years, from AD 793 to 1066. The Vikings became famous not just as warriors, but also as traders, sailors, craftsmen, storytellers, and explorers.

In the ninth century, the Vikings were on the move! Viking traders took their goods all the way to the lands now called Russia and Iraq. Viking warriors set out to raid up and down the coasts of Europe and England. Daring Viking explorers set off in search of new lands, and Viking families settled in places far from their homes in Scandinavia.

The Word *Viking*

The Vikings spoke a language that we call Old Norse. They didn't call themselves Vikings. They were known as Northmen.

The Old Norse word for "raider" is *vikingr*. When the Vikings sailed off on a raid, they said they were "going in Viking." Many years later, people began using the term *Viking* for Scandinavians who lived in the Age of the Vikings.

How We Know About the Vikings

The Vikings didn't leave behind many written records. Most couldn't read or write. For hundreds of years, they told stories about their kings and heroes. These stories are called *sagas*. On long winter nights, parents recited the sagas to their children. When the children grew up, they told the same sagas to their children.

People in Iceland began writing the sagas down in the twelfth century, long after the Age of the Vikings was over. Their writings

Viking jewelry

give details about the Vikings' weapons, customs, and beliefs.

Archaeologists have uncovered ships, graves, and even whole Viking towns. Many items such as pots, tools, and jewelry were buried at the sites. These are objects that the Vikings used every day. Some look a lot like things we still use.

Archaeologists find and study ancient objects to learn about people who lived many years ago.

Viking Society

There were three ranks of people in the Viking world. At the top were rich and powerful chieftains and kings.

In the middle were freemen. Freemen could own weapons, land, and slaves. They held meetings to vote on laws and to choose their chieftains and kings. These meetings were called the *Althingi*.

Slaves were captured or were born to parents who were slaves. They were the lowest rank and had no rights at all. They had to obey their owners and worked at hard jobs like spreading manure on fields or cleaning out barns.

2

Viking Warriors

Viking warriors were strong, daring, and brutal. They didn't think of themselves as robbers. They believed they were doing an important job to survive. A successful raider who returned with riches and captives was everyone's hero.

Viking warriors believed that Odin, the god of war and poetry, was their special god. For a Viking, the best death was to die fighting. Viking warriors thought if that happened, they would go to Valhalla, Odin's great feasting hall in the heavens.

Viking chieftains and kings owned big halls where they feasted with their warriors.

Raids

Vikings usually raided in the warmer spring and summer months. Then they would go back home when the weather got cold.

Early raids weren't with large armies and fleets of warships. At first, the Vikings used only a few ships and a small number of men.

Loot is anything that people steal.

Raids were not like well-planned battles. The men dashed in, killed people, destroyed buildings, and left with *loot* and captives.

This illustration of a Viking raid came from the book <u>The Church of England: A History for the People</u>.

Everything they took had to fit on the ship. The warriors grabbed tools, weapons, and clothing as well as gold and silver. They also butchered cattle and carried the meat back to the ship.

Attacks

As kings took more control in Scandinavia, the raids got bigger. Rulers gathered armies with thousands of men and fought real battles.

The Vikings sailed up rivers to

attack and loot cities. They traveled up the River Thames and attacked London several different times. Hundreds of ships and thousands of soldiers went up the Seine River to loot Paris.

 King Cnut was the first Viking king of England.

In AD 865, Vikings from Norway, Sweden, and Denmark formed one great Viking army to invade England. They stayed there for almost fifteen years.

During that time, the Vikings were able to control large parts of the country. They set up winter camps and held on to the land they'd conquered.

The Vikings also seized parts of

Scotland, Ireland, and France. Settlers arrived to live there. They set up farms and villages and began to prosper.

Two Famous Warriors

Legends are stories that have been passed down over the years. There are legends about famous Viking warriors. Two of them were Hastein and Ragnar Lodbrok.

Hastein was a Viking chieftain. He led his warriors on raids along the coasts of France and Spain. Once, Hastein attacked a town in Italy.

Hastein thought it was Rome. Wrong! It was a town called Luna.

There is one famous story that says when Hastein couldn't break through the town's walls, he sent a messenger to tell his enemies that he'd died and needed to be buried in a churchyard.

31

Hastein's men carried him into the church for burial. Suddenly, he leapt up, bashed his way to the gate, and let his men inside!

Another popular Viking hero, Ragnar Lodbrok, wore pants made from hairy animal skins. Lodbrok actually means *Hairy Breeches*. Ragnar thought he had a direct link to Odin and was hungry for power and fame.

Ragnar attacked Paris, but King Charles the Fat paid him money to leave the city alone. Later, Ragnar was shipwrecked off the coast of England. He survived, but the king of Northumbria captured him.

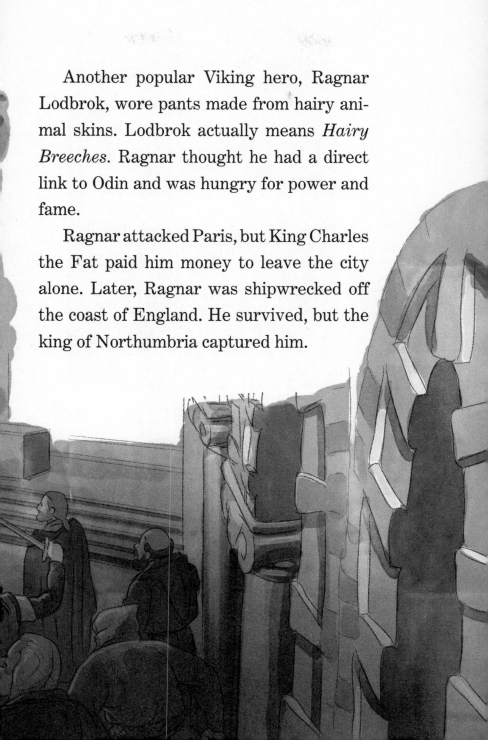

 Richard Henry Brock drew this picture of Ragnar's legendary death.

Some stories say the king threw Ragnar into a pit full of poisonous snakes. That was the end of Ragnar . . . and his hairy pants!

Later, Ragnar's sons, including Ivar the

Boneless, took revenge and shot the king full of arrows. And that was the end of the king of Northumbria!

Berserkers!

Warriors called berserkers were the scariest Viking fighters. Because they were so sure they would get to Valhalla, they were not afraid to die.

Berserkers went into a kind of weird trance when they fought. They didn't care about anything but killing.

Before a fight, a berserker would work himself into a rage. He'd bite his shield and howl like a bloodthirsty maniac. Then he would charge into battle—sometimes with nothing on but an animal skin cloak! Today "going berserk" means losing control and going absolutely bananas.

Viking Timeline

AD 793
Vikings raid the monastery at Lindisfarne.

AD 795
Vikings begin to attack Ireland.

AD 836
Warriors invade Wessex in Southern England.

AD 860s
Vikings settle in Iceland.

AD 865
Great Viking army invades England.

AD 876
Vikings from Norway, Sweden, and Denmark settle in England.

AD 885–886

Thousands of warriors attack Paris for ten months without success.

AD 1000

Leif Eriksson sails to North America.

AD 1014

King Cnut of Denmark becomes the English king.

AD 1016

Vikings defeated in England by King Harold II.

End of the Age of the Vikings . . . no more raids!

3

Ready for Battle

Vikings carried weapons with them almost everywhere they went. It was a custom for all kings, chieftains, and freemen to own them.

Swords were the most prized weapons. They were supposed to be the choice of heroes. Only the most powerful Vikings could afford them.

Warriors often gave their swords special names. One of the most popular was

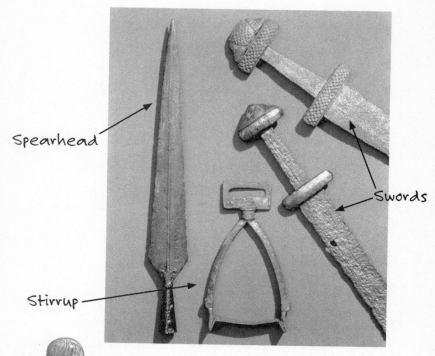

Spearhead

Swords

Stirrup

Some sword hilts had handsome silver, bronze, or copper designs on them.

Fotbitr, which meant "Leg Biter." Other names were things like Killer, Brain Biter, and Family Blade.

Viking warriors were usually buried with weapons.

Most warriors fought with spears and iron battle-axes. Spears were six to ten feet long. Vikings threw them at their enemies. They were also useful for stabbing people in hand-to-hand combat.

There are stories about warriors who threw two spears at the same time—one in each hand. Others were said to catch an incoming spear out of the air with their hands!

Battle-axes had longer handles than axes that the Vikings used for chopping wood. They were strong enough to cut through metal. And they were sharp enough to cut off arms and legs!

Battle-axes

Dressing Like a Warrior

Vikings didn't usually wear armor. They fought in padded leather tunics that came down to their knees. Their shoes were leather, and they wore long woolen socks. Sometimes they wound strips of leather over the socks.

If a warrior could afford it, he might wear a chain-mail shirt as his armor. It was made of thousands of metal rings hooked together.

King Magnus Barefoot wears a mail shirt in this illustration of his final battle.

Pictures of Vikings wearing helmets with horns on them are wrong. Not one horned helmet has ever been found!

Some warriors wore iron helmets with nose and eye guards. Most of the men wore leather helmets.

Vikings protected themselves with large, round wooden shields painted in bold colors like yellow, red, or black.

This copy of a Viking shield shows how the real ones were decorated.

Boys learned how to use weapons and fight when they were young. There are some graves with warriors as young as sixteen who died in battle.

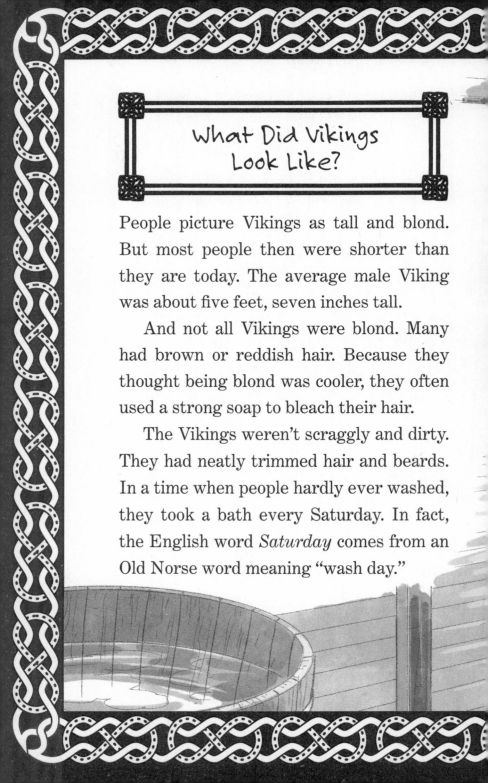

What Did Vikings Look Like?

People picture Vikings as tall and blond. But most people then were shorter than they are today. The average male Viking was about five feet, seven inches tall.

And not all Vikings were blond. Many had brown or reddish hair. Because they thought being blond was cooler, they often used a strong soap to bleach their hair.

The Vikings weren't scraggly and dirty. They had neatly trimmed hair and beards. In a time when people hardly ever washed, they took a bath every Saturday. In fact, the English word *Saturday* comes from an Old Norse word meaning "wash day."

4

The Longship

The Vikings built great boats. The most famous were longships. They were strong enough to sail through the roughest seas. Longships were faster than any other ships of the time.

These great ships made the Vikings successful. Warriors were able to attack places and get away quickly. They helped Viking traders sail as far away as Russia and Iraq. And Viking families crossed the seas in them to settle in different lands.

Dragon and Serpent Heads

Longships were long and narrow with curved fronts and backs. Since they were the same shape at both ends, they went backward as easily as forward.

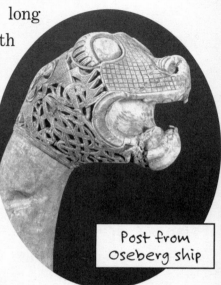

Post from Oseberg ship

Replica dragon head

Some ships had carved dragon or serpent heads on their prow, or front. The Vikings probably had them for good luck. And they also looked very frightening!

One famous ship was named *The Long Serpent*. Others were *Snake of the Sea* and *Raven of the Wind*.

Prow of Oseberg ship

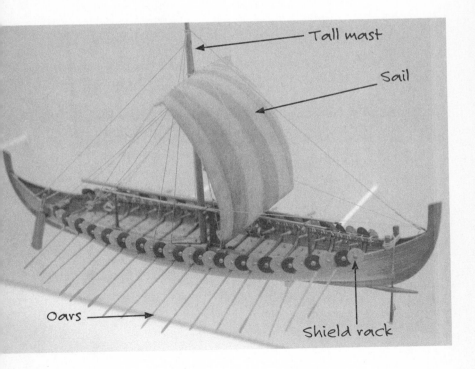

Tall mast

Sail

Oars

Shield rack

People in Iceland believed that land spirits lived in special places on their island. They made a rule that only ships without serpent or dragon heads could enter their waters. They worried that the land spirits would get upset!

Building Longships

Viking ships were light and strong. They were specially built to support the tall masts and large sails needed for speed. They were also very stable.

Viking shipbuilders used long, narrow planks that overlapped each other. They helped keep the ships from breaking apart in strong seas.

Viking ships were light enough to move through shallow water right up to the shore. Some could even get through as little as

Ships built this way are called <u>clinker-built</u> ships.

twenty inches of water with no trouble!

Other ships couldn't do this without the bottom of the ship getting stuck in the sand. Their sailors first had to anchor in deep waters offshore. Then they climbed into small boats and rowed to shore. The Vikings could zip in from the open ocean and strike like lightning.

The builders waterproofed the decks with tar. A rack on the side of the ship held the warriors' shields. The shield rack also protected the sides of the ship.

Sails

There was one large square sail made of wool or linen. The sailors could take it down when they didn't need it.

The sails may have been red or red and white.

Only small
pieces of sails
have ever been
found.

The sails cost a lot—almost as much as the ship itself. Weavers wove long oblong strips of cloth on very large looms. They sewed the strips together and

This Norwegian woman still weaves on the kind of loom Viking weavers would have used.

coated them with animal fat to water-proof them.

Wind blowing into the sail moved the ship forward. At top speed, a longship traveled about eight to ten miles an hour.

Turn the page to read about the most famous Viking explorers!

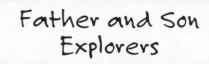

Father and Son Explorers

Today, the two most famous Viking explorers are Erik the Red and Leif Eriksson. Erik was known for his red beard and hot temper. Around AD 981, he was sent away from his home in Iceland for killing someone.

Erik sailed hundreds of miles west until he reached an unknown island. He spent three years there. When he returned to Iceland, he convinced others to settle the new island with him. To make it sound pleasant, he called it Greenland. Erik became a rich and powerful chieftain and lived the rest of his days there. The Viking colony in Greenland lasted for over five hundred years.

Erik's son, Leif Eriksson, was also a great sailor. But in AD 999, when Leif was returning from Norway, his ship blew off course. He and his crew finally landed in what was probably Newfoundland, Canada. The men found lush green fields with wild grapevines growing everywhere.

Leif named his discovery Vinland for its vines. He spent the winter there before going back to Greenland. Leif had landed in North America five hundred years before Christopher Columbus!

At L'Anse aux Meadows in Newfoundland, archaeologists have restored Norse longhouses.

5

Life on Board

When the Vikings were near land, they camped under the stars. Most of the time, however, they lived on their ships.

The men sailed and rowed through rain, cold, and high winds. They wrapped up in wool blankets for warmth. At night, the sailors could take down the sail and use it like a big tent.

Since they couldn't cook on board the ship, they ate dried fish and fruit, plus hard, crisp bread that tasted like a cracker.

Rowing

When the wind died or the water was shallow, the men rowed. They sat on sea chests that held their belongings and rowed in shifts. One shift probably lasted two to three hours. During that time, sailors could take as many as a thousand strokes!

Yikes! There were no bathrooms on the ships. The men went over the sides.

The longest Viking ship ever found
was in Denmark. It was 119 feet long

and held about 100 men and 72 oars. This ship could make it through water only three feet deep without dragging on the bottom!

Steering

One sailor steered the boat with a long wooden oar. The steering oar is called the starboard oar. It was attached to the right side of the ship with a leather strap. The right side was easier for right-handed sailors.

Today, the right side of a ship is the starboard side. Can you guess why?

Vikings often used whale and seal skins for rope.

The sailor who steered was the *helmsman*. He guided the ship by moving the starboard oar to the left or right. Another sailor was a lookout. He stood at the front to check for rocks and other dangers. His job was to tell the helmsman what lay ahead.

Navigation

Although Viking ships didn't have compasses or maps, they may have had small sundials. They also may have used a crystal called a sunstone to see the position of the sun on a cloudy day.

Mostly they *navigated* using nature as their guide. To figure out direction, the sailors looked at where the sun and stars were in the sky. The sun rises in the east and sets in the west. At night, the bright North Star showed them which way was north.

To <u>navigate</u> means to find your way.

The men also knew the seabirds and whales that lived in certain parts of the sea. The color of the water gave them clues as well. Water in the deep ocean looks very dark blue. It gets lighter the closer you get to land.

Sailing was in the Vikings' blood, but it took years to learn how to sail well. Fathers passed this knowledge down to their sons. Just imagine how amazing it must have been to see certain birds or whales and know where you were in the ocean!

A Viking Burial

The Vikings believed in life after death. They often had things buried with them to use in the afterlife.

In 1880, some Norwegian brothers found a thousand-year-old longship on the family farm in Gokstad. The ship was about seventy-six feet long. Inside was the skeleton of a warrior. It showed he'd died from battle wounds to his legs.

Buried with him were sixty-four shields, six beds, a tent, a game board, three small boats, and the remains of twelve horses, six dogs, two hawks, and two peacocks!

In 1893, the Norwegians built a ship just like the Gokstad. They sailed it across the

Atlantic Ocean to North America. The ship did well and averaged about ten miles an hour. Some people said that it was the most beautiful thing they'd ever seen.

In 1893, the <u>Viking</u>, a replica of the Gokstad ship, sailed from Norway to Chicago.

6

Religion

Vikings held festivals on certain days of the year. Many of these were to honor their gods. They had gods for a good harvest, war, the sea, love, poetry, winter, and wisdom. There was also a goddess of skiing! Her name was Skadi.

Viking myths are most often called Norse myths.

The Vikings prayed to their gods for good weather, success in battles, wealth, and much more. To please them, people offered sacrifices of animals such as oxen, horses, goats, and sometimes even human beings.

The Vikings probably didn't worship in special buildings like churches or temples. Instead, they seem to have worshipped at rocks, near waterfalls, and in special groves of trees where they felt the spirits of the gods might be.

The Myth of Yggdrasil and Asgard

The Vikings thought the world was flat and that a huge ocean surrounded it. Many myths tell of a huge yew tree named Yggdrasil (IG-druh-sill). It was so massive that its branches could hold up the entire world. The gods were thought to meet and hold court at Yggdrasil every day.

The Vikings believed the heavenly home of the gods was in Asgard. It could only be

Yggdrasil

reached by crossing a rainbow bridge up to
the heavens.

Odin's great hall, Valhalla, was in Asgard.
Some myths say that Valhalla's walls were

This engraving of Valhalla is from a 1912 book.

made of gleaming spears and that the roof was made of shields that glowed in the dark.

Every night, Odin and his dead warriors feasted together on the meat of a wild boar. The same boar would magically reappear on the table the next night.

Viking myths tell of gods in bloody battles with dragons, monsters, and giants. A few of the myths are funny, but most of them are dark and filled with violence.

Sail along with us to discover our favorite Norse gods and goddesses.

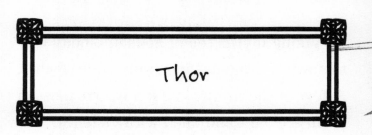

Thor

The most popular god was Thor, Odin's son. Thor had great strength and controlled thunder, lightning, and giant storms. People pictured him as having a flaming red beard and a huge hammer.

Thor raced across the heavens in a chariot pulled by two goats. As the chariot barreled along, it made thunder shake the earth. When Thor threw his hammer, dazzling streaks of lightning flashed across the sky. Each time he tossed it, the hammer whizzed right back to him.

To honor Thor, Vikings often wore necklaces with little hammers on them. The word *Thursday* comes from Thor's name. And guess what? It means "thunder's day"!

Freyr

Beautiful Freyr was the god of the harvest, wealth, and peace. Farmers prayed that Freyr would give them many healthy children and rain and sunshine for their crops to grow.

Freyr sailed on a magical ship big enough to hold all the gods and their weapons. Since a strong wind always blew behind its sails, his was the fastest ship of all.

When he finished sailing, Freyr would fold up his ship, put it in a small pouch, and slip it into his pocket. Freyr rode on the back of a huge golden boar with bristles that shone like rays of the sun.

Loki

Loki was a shape changer and a trickster. He could turn into animals like fish, horses, and falcons. At times, Loki helped the gods, but his tricks also made them angry.

Once, the gods were having a feast and didn't invite Loki. He reminded Odin of a promise that they would always drink together.

Odin gave in and invited Loki to join the party. Loki was horrible! He insulted the gods. He called them bad names and had terrible manners.

The gods tried to throw him out, but Loki escaped. He fled to a stream and turned himself into a salmon. At night, he came back onshore.

When the gods found him, Loki turned himself back into a salmon and tried to leap into the water. The gods threw out a net and caught that old trickster in midair!

Frigg

Frigg was the goddess of married women and love. She was also Odin's wife and queen of Asgard. Frigg and Odin had a son named Baldr. He was a beautiful god of light and purity.

Loki was jealous of Baldr. One day he changed into an old woman and visited Frigg. He tricked her into telling him a big secret. She whispered to Loki that only mistletoe could kill her beloved Baldr.

Loki fooled a blind god named Hod into throwing a dart of mistletoe at Baldr. It hit him right in the heart, and he died.

All the gods and even the giants came to Baldr's funeral. They gently put his body in a boat. Then a giantess came riding in on a wolf and pushed the ship out to sea.

Freyja and the Valkyries

Freyja was the goddess of love and beauty. She was also the goddess of battle and death. Wearing a coat made of falcon feathers, she drove a chariot pulled by two large gray cats.

Everything about Freyja was lovely. She sang sweet love songs and cried golden tears. Everywhere she went, she scattered sparkling dewdrops on the ground.

Some myths say that Freyja led the Valkyries, Odin's women warriors. The Valkyries chose which warriors would die in combat.

After a battle, they carried half of all who died up to Valhalla. The rest went to Freyja and spent their afterlives in her beautiful field.

7

Viking Farms

At home, the Vikings usually lived on lonely farms far from any neighbors. Big families often lived together. Sometimes ten to twenty people shared the same house! If the husband was away, his wife took charge of the farm.

A Viking house, called a longhouse, was shaped like a rectangle. Its walls were made of wood, stone, or hard blocks of dirt, grass, and roots, called turf. Wood, turf, or straw roofs kept out the rain and cold. When there was a turf roof, the grass spread out until it covered the whole house!

The Vikings had a custom of planting a special tree near their house. They felt it protected them and honored the spirits of their dead relatives.

Most houses were one long room. Benches lined the walls. The family sat on them during the day. At night, they covered the benches with soft blankets and turned them into beds.

A large open fire pit was in the middle of the room. It gave off the heat and light. Women cooked over the fire, and smoke escaped through a hole in the roof.

Sometimes a barn was attached to the house.

In the winter, the family dressed warmly and sat huddled close to the warmth of the fire. After dinner, people told stories and played board games that were a lot like checkers or chess. Vikings also liked to sing and tell riddles.

There were no windows in Viking longhouses. Light came from the fire and lamps burning animal fat or grasses and straw. The houses were dark, and the

walls were covered in soot. At times, it must have been hard to breathe.

Farmwork

People died young then, many of lung diseases like tuberculosis— possibly from the smoke in their homes.

The biggest job for a farmer was making sure there was enough food for everyone. There were no Viking grocery stores! Most of the things people needed to survive, they made themselves.

90

Farmers often raised sheep, pigs, goats, and cattle. Their farm animals gave them milk, cheese, butter, and meat.

Farmers also grew wheat, barley, and other crops.

They also got meat by hunting deer, rabbits, and elk with their bows and arrows. If the family lived near the water, fish made up a large part of their diet.

Women and girls spent hours weaving wool or linen on looms. They made animal skins, fur, and wool into warm clothing.

Linen cloth was made from the fibers of the flax plant.

People carved animal bones into knives, buttons, needles, drinking cups, and ice skate blades.

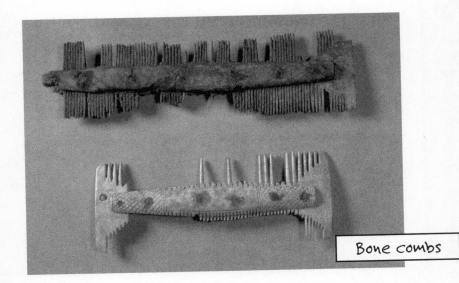

Bone combs

Viking Kids

Viking kids grew up quickly. By the time they were twelve, they were treated as adults. There were no schools, so kids worked all day.

If you were a Viking farm boy, you had to:

Work in the fields

Hunt animals

Cut wood for fires

Catch fish

Practice with weapons

Fathers showed their sons how to manage the farm. Since most girls married when they were teenagers, they learned how to run a house when they were very young.

If you were a Viking farm girl, you had to:

Cook on a fire

Sew and weave

Take care of the younger children

Clean the house

Milk cows

Cooking and Food

The Vikings ate twice a day, in the morning and at night. Women cooked in large pots called cauldrons that hung over the fire.

People didn't use forks. They carried a knife and a spoon in a pouch on their belt. Everyone ate from wooden bowls and plates.

The family sat down to meals of meat, fish, porridge, and vegetables like cabbage, turnips, beans, and onions. The favorite drinks were beer made from barley and mead made from honey.

For special occasions, Vikings drank from a drinking horn.

To keep meat or fish from spoiling in the summer, the Vikings smoked or pickled it with salt. They also hung it outside to dry.

Clothes

Kids dressed like their parents. Sometimes women dyed the clothes in bright colors like red, blue, purple, and yellow.

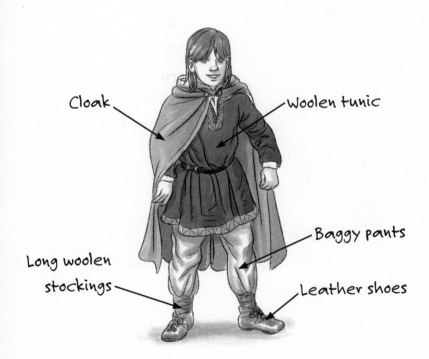

Cloak

Woolen tunic

Baggy pants

Long woolen stockings

Leather shoes

Shawl or cloak

Apron

Ankle-length dress

Leather shoes

Fun

Kids didn't work all the time. In their free time, they played with whistles, tops, toy boats, and wooden swords. In the winter, there was ice skating, skiing, and sledding.

If they wanted to play ball, they had to make their own! They soaked wool in water and squeezed it out over and over again until it became hard enough to make into a ball.

Names

Parents gave boys first names like Dag, Knut, or Leif. Common names for girls were Helga, Ingibjörg, or Astrid.

Vikings didn't have last names. A boy was known as the son of his father. That's why Erik the Red's son was called Leif Eriksson.

Girls were known as daughters of their father. If a girl had a father named Erik, she would be called Eriksdottir.

Many Vikings had nicknames. There was Svein Forkbeard, Hergrim Half-Troll, Ulf Squint-Eye, and Thorunn Blue-Cheek. And let's not leave out Ketil Flatnose!

If you were a Viking, what would your name be? And what would your nickname be?

My nickname would be Annie Animal-Hugger.

And mine could be Jack Round-Glasses!

Vikings were loyal to their families. Since there were no policemen, people needed their families for protection.

If someone hurt a family member, the family would take revenge. Sometimes they killed someone from the other family or burned his house down! Family fights often lasted for years.

The Vikings endured lives full of hardship. There were no doctors or hospitals. Children often died before their fifth birthday. Adults usually died in their thirties or forties. It was often because of their families that so many people managed to live even that long.

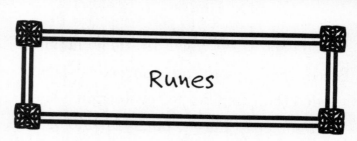

Runes

The Vikings didn't write on paper. They didn't have any. They did have an alphabet with twenty-four symbols called runes. The runes looked like sticks.

They carved runes on wood, stone, and animal bones. Craftsmen or boatbuilders carved their names into things they'd built.

Sometimes people carved runes on large stones and put them on roadways. They might say things like "Canute built this road and owns this land."

Not all Vikings understood what the runes said. Some are even written in code. A bone with a coded rune was discovered in Sweden. Someone figured out that it says "Kiss me"!

Rune stone near
Stockholm, Sweden

8

End of an Age

For about three hundred years, the Vikings changed the history of Europe and England. And then the Vikings themselves began to change.

Kings from other countries had armies that could fight off the Vikings. In 1066, England's King Harold Godwinson defeated King Harald Hardraade of Norway. This defeat almost ended all of the Viking invasions. By the 1100s, the Viking raids had come to an end.

Becoming Christians

The Vikings slowly started to believe in Christianity. Many had settled in Christian lands like England, Ireland, and France. Viking kings became Christians as well and saw that their people did, too. By the end

The Vikings built many wooden churches like this one, called a stave church.

of the twelfth century, most of the Vikings
had given up their old gods.

Language

Perhaps one of the Vikings' greatest gifts
was the hundreds of English words that
come from the Old Norse language. There
are words that we use every day like
egg, *get*, *club*, *take*, *bug*, and *freckle*. And
many English words that begin with *sk*
come from Old Norse. How many can you
write down?

Myths and Sagas

Viking storytellers and poets made their
living telling stories and reciting poems.
They wandered the land from one celebra-
tion to another and were welcomed guests.

There are still stories about Vikings
everywhere—on TV, in movies, in comics,

and in operas. There's even a football team called the Minnesota Vikings!

People enjoy festivals where they can dress up like Vikings and eat food like the Vikings would have eaten. Some Viking admirers have built and sailed longships just like the ones from long ago.

Opening the World

Viking explorers, settlers, and traders opened up the world. By settling in new places, they brought different cultures together.

Today, there are remains of Viking towns in many places, especially England and Ireland. Their Norse names give them away. If the town's name ends in *by*, as in Whitby, you know that Vikings once lived there. There are over two hundred towns and villages in northern England ending in these letters.

So even though the great Age of the Vikings has been over for hundreds of years, in many ways the Vikings are still with us today.

Doing More Research

There's a lot more you can learn about Vikings. The fun of research is seeing how many different sources you can explore.

Books

Most libraries and bookstores have books about Vikings.

Here are some things to remember when you're using books for research:

1. You don't have to read the whole book. Check the table of contents and the index to find the topics you're interested in.

2. Write down the name of the book.

When you take notes, make sure you write down the name of the book in your notebook so you can find it again.

3. Never copy exactly from a book.

When you learn something new from a book, put it in your own words.

4. Make sure the book is <u>nonfiction</u>.

Some books tell make-believe stories about Vikings. Make-believe stories are called *fiction*. They're fun to read, but not good for research.

Research books have facts and tell true stories. They are called *nonfiction*. A librarian or teacher can help you make sure the books you use for research are nonfiction.

Here are some good nonfiction books about Vikings:

- *Life on a Viking Ship* by Jane Shuter
- *The Real Vikings* by Melvin Berger and Gilda Berger
- *Viking* (DK Eyewitness Books) by Susan M. Margeson
- *Viking Tales* by Jennie Hall
- *Vikings* by Phil Wilkinson
- *What Did the Vikings Do for Me?* by Elizabeth Raum

Museums

Many museums can help you learn more about Vikings.

When you go to a museum:

1. Be sure to take your notebook!
Write down anything that catches your interest. Draw pictures, too!

2. Ask questions.
There are almost always people at museums who can help you find what you're looking for.

3. Check the calendar.
Many museums have special events and activities just for kids!

Here are some museums with exhibits about Vikings:

- Field Museum (Chicago)
- Maine Maritime Museum (Bath)
- Mariners' Museum (Newport News, Virginia)
- Maritime Museum of the Atlantic (Halifax, Nova Scotia)
- Metropolitan Museum of Art (New York City)
- National Museum of Natural History, Smithsonian Institution (Washington, D.C.)

The Internet

Many websites have lots of facts about Vikings. Some also have games and activities that can help make learning about Vikings even more fun.

Ask your teacher or your parents to help you find more websites like these:

- bbc.co.uk/schools/primaryhistory/vikings
- ducksters.com/history/middle_ages _timeline.php
- fun-facts.org.uk/vikings/vikings.htm
- getthespecialists.co.uk/101_Viking _Facts.html
- history.com/news/history-lists/10-things -you-may-not-know-about-the-vikings

- kidskonnect.com/history/vikings
- ngkids.co.uk/history/10_facts_about_the
  _vikings
- rmg.co.uk/explore/sea-and-ships/facts
  /ships-and-seafarers/the-vikings
- topicpod.com/vikings/what_viking
  _weapons.html

Good luck!

Index

Have you read the adventure that matches up with this book?

Don't miss Magic Tree House® #15
Viking Ships at Sunrise

Jack and Annie are whisked back to ancient Ireland—just in time for a Viking invasion!

If you're looking forward to
Magic Tree House® #54:
Balto of the Blue Dawn
you'll love finding out the facts
behind the fiction in
**Magic Tree House®
Fact Tracker**

DOGSLEDDING AND EXTREME SPORTS

A nonfiction companion to
Magic Tree House® #54:
Balto of the Blue Dawn

It's Jack and Annie's very own guide
to dogsledding and other extreme sports.
Coming soon!

Magic Tree House® Books

Merlin Missions

Magic Tree House® Fact Trackers

More Magic Tree House®